How to Draw Zombies Step-by-Step Guide

Best Zombie Drawing Book for You and Your Kids

BY

ANDY HOPPER

© 2019 Andy Hopper All Rights Reserved

Copyright Notes

The material in question, hereto referred to as The Book, may not be reproduced in any part by any means without the explicit permission of the bearer of the material, hereto known as the Author. Reproduction of The Book includes (but is not limited to) any printed copies, electronic copies, scanned copies or photocopies.

The Book was written as an informational guide and nothing more. The Reader assumes any and all risk when following the suggestions or guidelines found therein. The Author has taken all precautions at ensuring accuracy in The Book but assumes no responsibility if any damage is caused by misinterpretation of the information contained therein.

Table of Contents

Introduction 4

Ballerina zombie 5

Zombie eating brain 32

Zombie's hand 53

Zombie Marilyn 75

Zombie in ripped jeans 94

The Walking dead 120

About the Author 141

Introduction

Kids have this intense desire to express themselves the ways they know how to. During their formative years, drawing all sorts is on top of their favorite things to do. You ought to encourage as it boosts their creativity and generally advances their cognitive development.

This book is written to give you and your kids the smoothest drawing experience with the different guides and instructions on how to draw different kinds of objects and animals. However, you should note that drawing, like everything worthwhile, requires a great deal of patience and consistency. Be patient with your kids as they wade through the tips and techniques in this book and put them into practice. Now, they will not get everything on the first try, but do not let this deter them. Be by their side at every step of the way and gently encourage them. In no time, they will be perfect little creators, and you, their trainer.

Besides, this is a rewarding activity to do as it presents you the opportunity of hanging out with your kids and connecting with them in ways you never knew was possible. The book contains all the help you need, now sit down with them and help them do this.

That is pretty much all about it - we should start this exciting journey now, shouldn't we?

Ballerina zombie

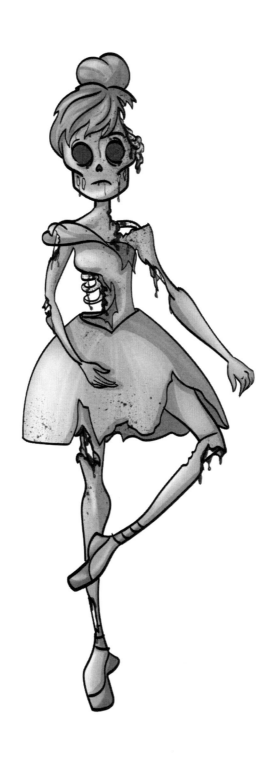

STEP 01

Draw a circle as her head shape.

STEP 02

Now we'll draw her jaw like this.

STEP 03

After that add a small rectangle as her neck;

[8]

STEP 04

And draw a slim body as shown.

STEP 05

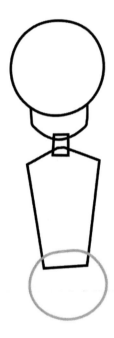

Add a circle as the base shape of her hip.

[10]

STEP 06

Let's draw her legs. First draw a carrot shape as her right thigh;

STEP 07

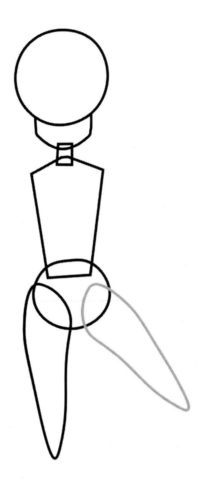

And another one for the other thigh.

STEP 08

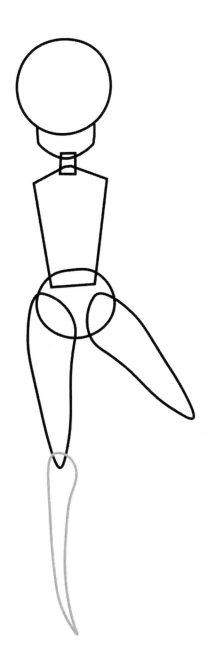

It's time to draw her leg as you can see in the picture.

STEP 09

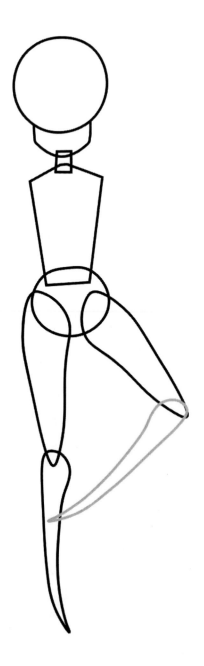

Repeat the previous step for the other leg.

[14]

STEP 10

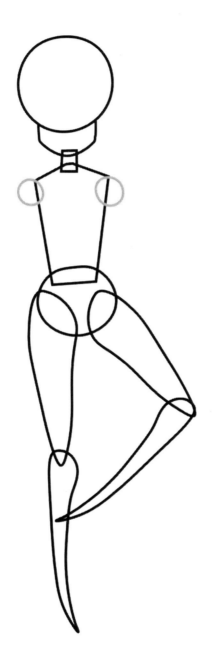

We should draw two small circles as her shoulders.

STEP 11

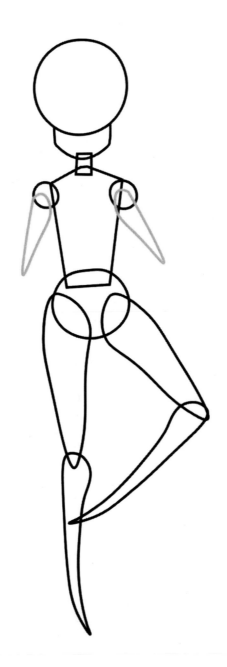

And two other carrot shapes (smaller than the thighs) as her biceps.

STEP 12

Now draw her forearms;

STEP 13

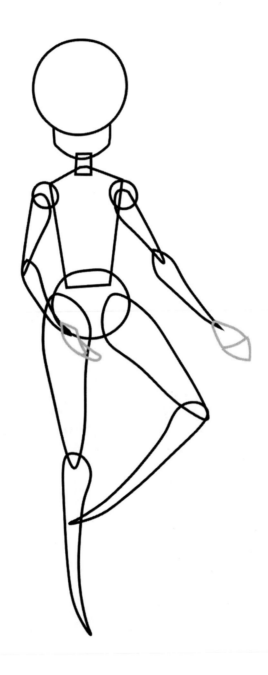

And her hands as well.

STEP 14

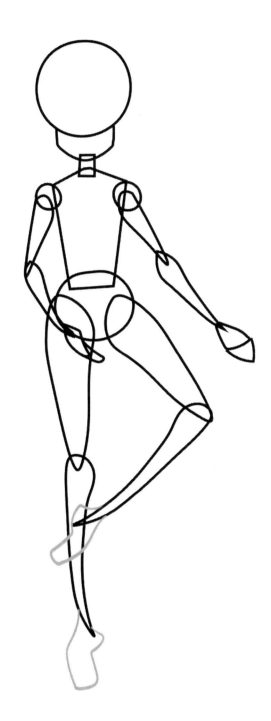

Now we just have to draw her ballet shoes and that's it!

STEP 15

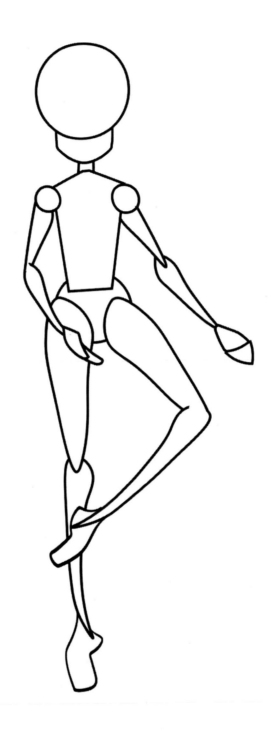

At this step I have removed some extra lines to show the base shape. You can scape this step if you want to.

STEP 16

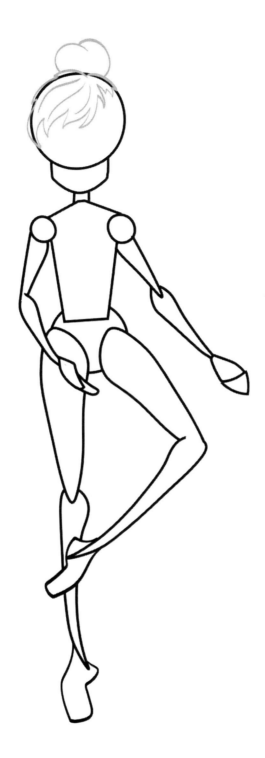

Let's draw a nice bun for her (you can choose another hair style).

STEP 17

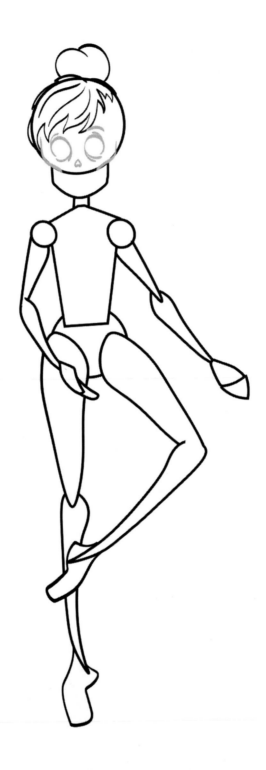

And we'll draw her face here…

[22]

STEP 18

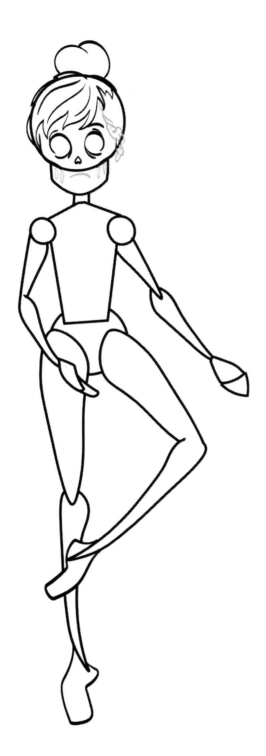

We can draw some wounds on her head since she is a zombie.

STEP 19

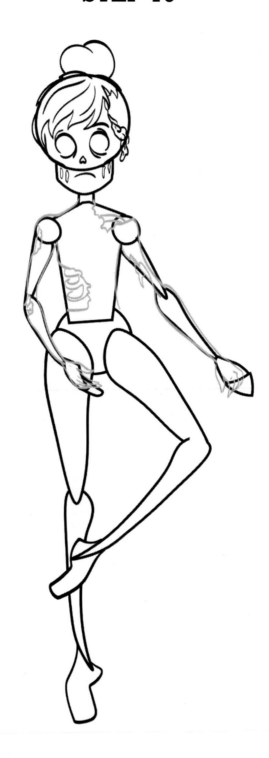

Now draw her upper body. I have drawn a big wound on her chest that made her ribs visible.

STEP 20

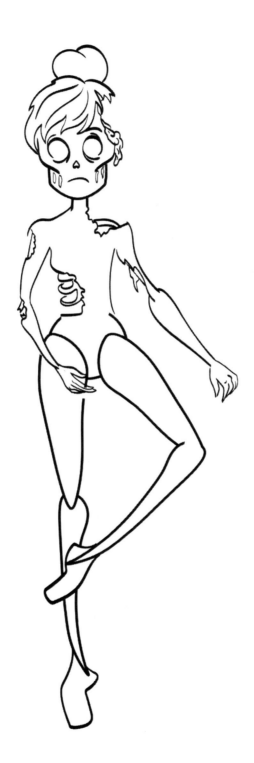

Let's remove the guide lines of her head and upper body.

STEP 21

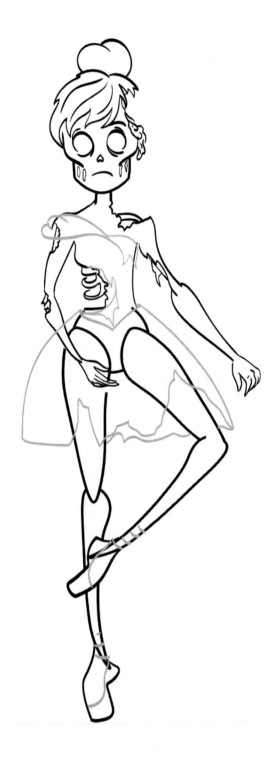

Of course she'll need a nice ballet dress! But unfortunately it's ripped off...

STEP 22

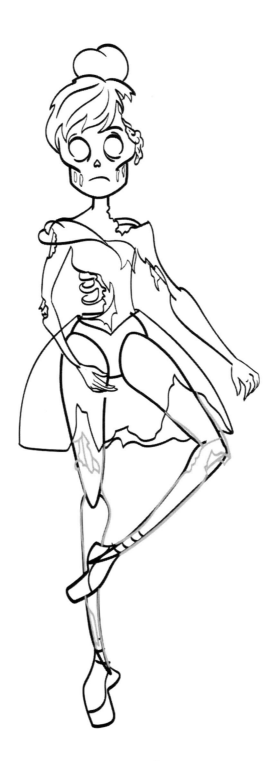

Draw her thin legs and some wounds on it;

STEP 23

And remove the guide lines of her legs. Your art line is done.

STEP 24

Let's color the drawing. I decided to make her dress dusty pink

STEP 25

Lights and shadows as always...

STEP 26

And draw a scene for her to perform her zombie ballet!

Zombie eating brain

STEP 01

We'll start our zombie with a circle as his head.

STEP 02

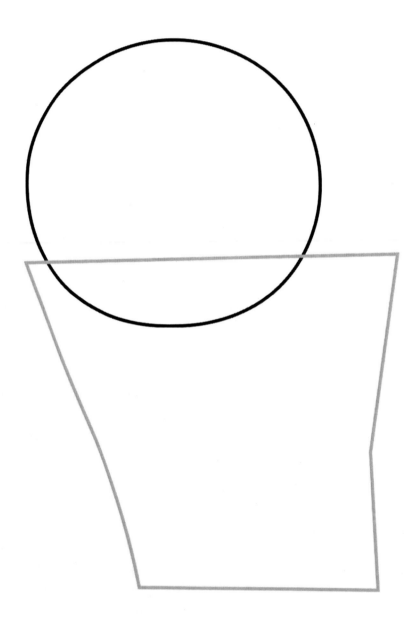

And continue with a trapezoid as his body.

STEP 03

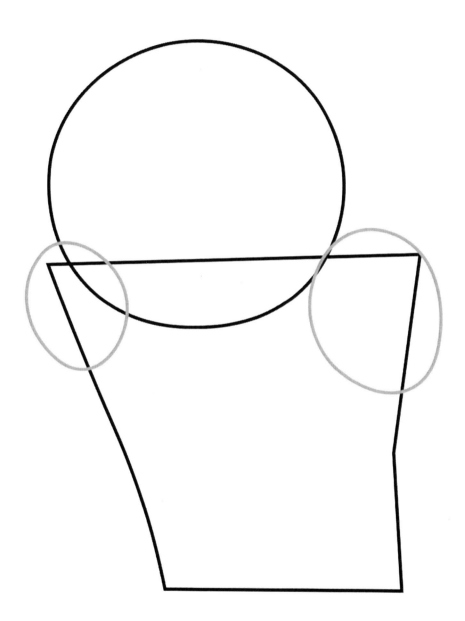

Let's add two circles to be his shoulders.

STEP 04

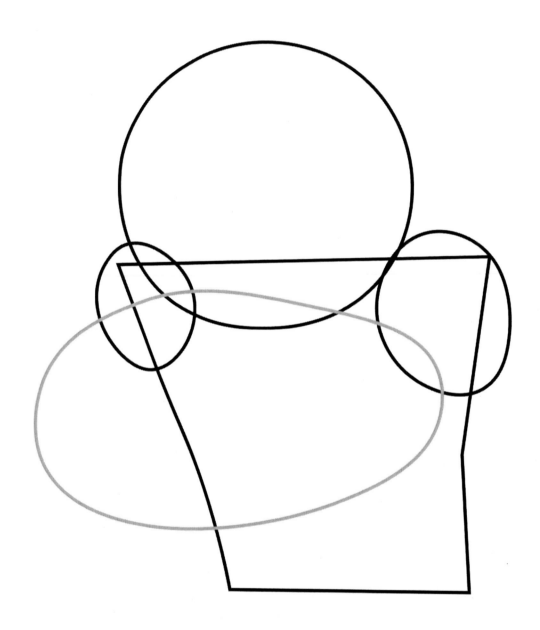

As I said we're drawing a zombie which is eating a brain, so let's draw a big oval circle as a big brain!

STEP 05

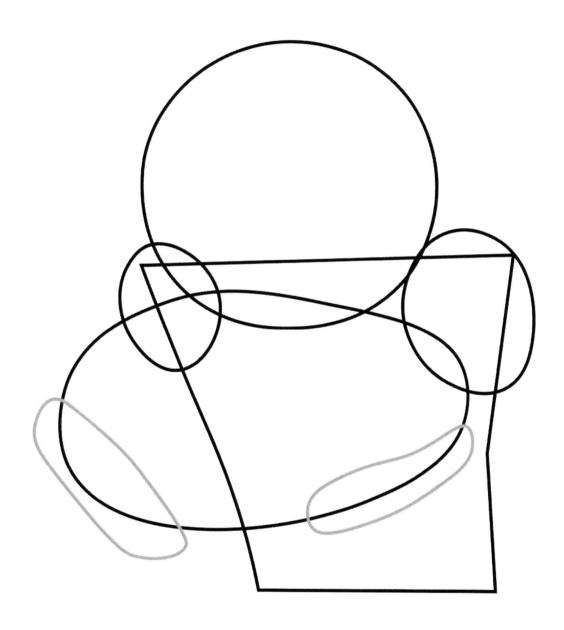

Draw two sausage-like shapes as his hands which are holding the big brain.

STEP 06

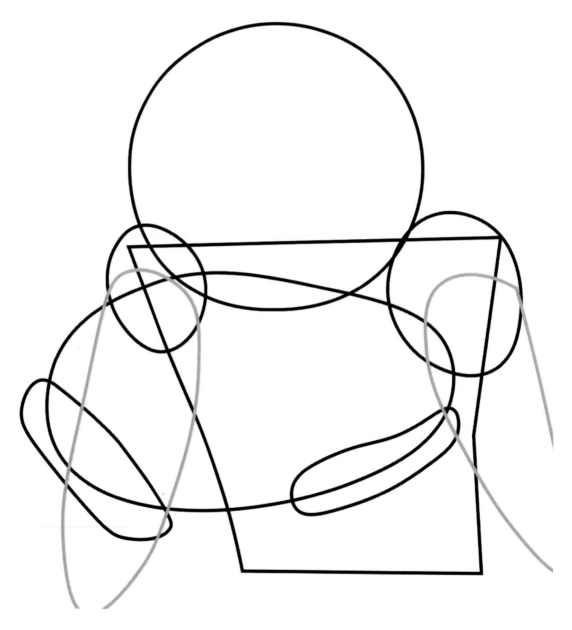

Look at the sample and draw his thin biceps as I did.

STEP 07

Erase the extra lines so that you can see the base shape of your zombie!

STEP 08

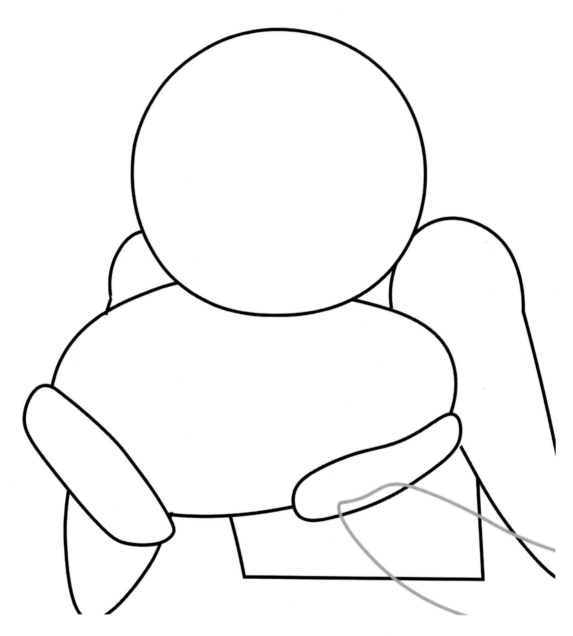

Now let's connect his left bicep to his hand by drawing his forearm;

STEP 09

And do the same for the other hand.

STEP 10

It's time to add some detail to his face!

STEP 11

And maybe some cracks on his skull and a worm which is living there to make him a little spookier...

STEP 12

Remove the head extra lines to reveal his evil face!

STEP 13

Draw some little sausages as the base shapes of his fingers.

[45]

STEP 14

Now that you have some guide lines to help you; you can draw his fingers easily.

STEP 15

Erase the extra lines again. We're almost done…

STEP 16

Add some details to the brain. I have drawn some of the brain between his fingers to show that the zombie is squishing it.

STEP 17

Erase the guide lines, and you'll have your art line done.

STEP 18

Let's put some color into our drawings!

STEP 19

Some shadows and highlights will be neede as well…

STEP 20

And to make it perfect just draw a background for it.

Zombie's hand

STEP 01

Let's start with a trapezoid as our zombie's forearm.

STEP 02

Then draw an oval circle upon the trapezoid as the wrist;

STEP 03

And we continue by drawing another oval as the parts of his palm which are visible.

STEP 04

Let's get to the fingers! We start with the index finger; draw two small circles as the joints and connect them by drawing two lines.

STEP 05

Repeat the previous step for the middle finger.

STEP 06

We have the ring finger at this step;

STEP 07

And draw two tiny circles as his pinkie finger's joints.

STEP 08

Finally, we draw his thumb and we have the base shape of our zombie hand!

STEP 09

At this step we start our refined drawing. Look at the picture and draw his thumb and index finger (bend the fingers so it seems that he had clenched his hand).

STEP 10

We can erase the extra lines.

STEP 11

Look at the picture and draw his middle finger;

STEP 12

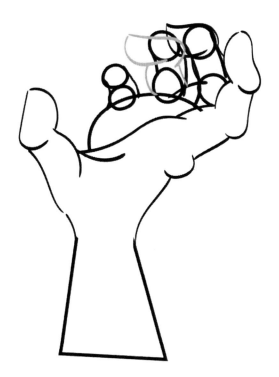

His ring finger;

STEP 13

And his pinkie as well.

STEP 14

Remove the extra lines once again. We have drawn a hand!

STEP 15

Let's add some details; draw some big scary nails and some fine lines on his hand to show the stretches on his hand.

STEP 16

He's coming out of the grave! Let's draw some soil to show it.

STEP 17

And don't forget about the tombstone.

STEP 18

Erase the extra lines and it's done!

STEP 19

Pick up your color pencils and color your drawing! I'll make mine green, you can choose any other color as well.

STEP 20

Some light and shadow will make it better...

STEP 21

And finally for background, let's draw a spooky night which made the dead bodies rise!

Zombie Marilyn

STEP 01

First we should draw a circle as her head.

STEP 02

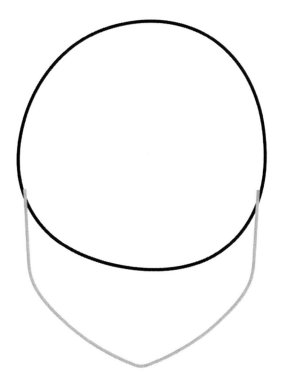

Then we'll draw her jaw and chin...

STEP 03

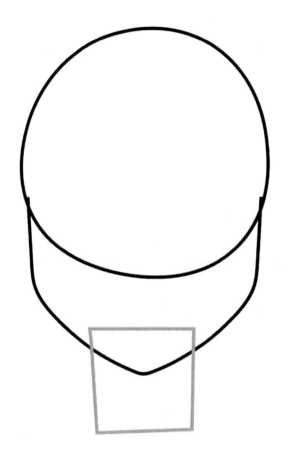

And a rectangle as her neck.

STEP 04

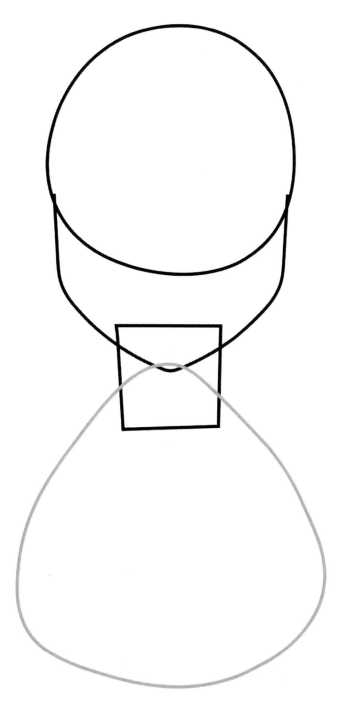

I have drawn a fat drop shape as her chest.

STEP 05

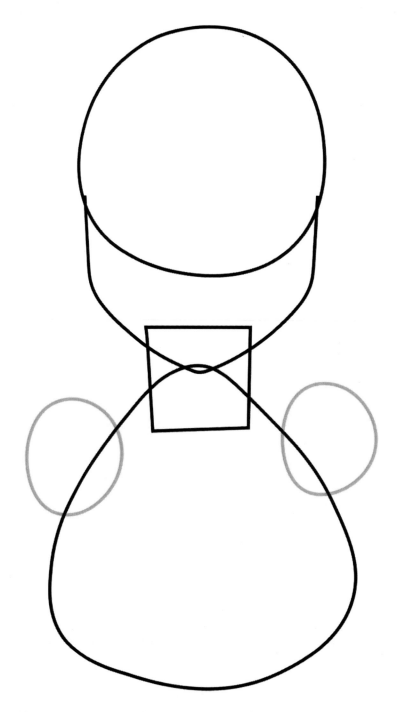

We should add two circles to be her shoulders.

STEP 06

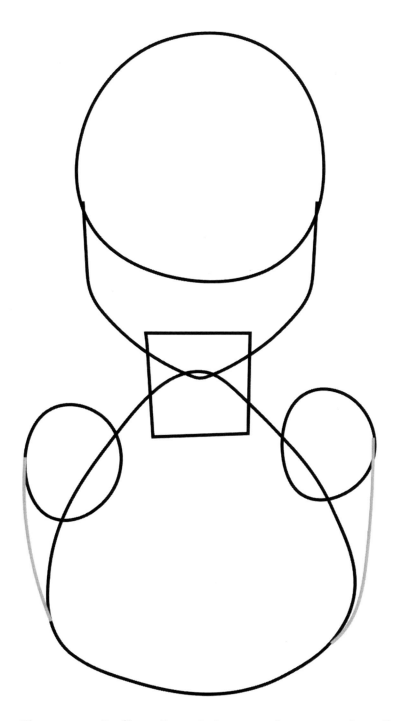

Draw two lines to define her biceps, just as simple as that!

STEP 07

Let's draw her beautiful wavy hair. I have left some parts hairless to draw a wound there later (since she's a zombie and her body can't be unharmed).

STEP 08

We should remove the extra lines. It looks good, isn't it?

STEP 09

Now it's time draw her face.

STEP 10

And put some wounds and scratches on her face (I know it's hard but we have to…).

STEP 11

If you look carefully you'll see some of her teeth is revealed from the big wound on her face.

STEP 12

Remove the extra lines around her jaw, and her face is done.

STEP 13

At this step we'll draw her dress and connect her neck to the shoulders.

STEP 14

Now add some more details and wounds on her body (look at the picture and do the same steps as I did).

STEP 15

Now you just have to remove the extra lines of her body to finish your drawing!

STEP 16

Let's color our beautiful Marilyn.

STEP 17

Don't forget the shadows and lights...

STEP 18

And finally, I have painted a beautiful sky full of stars for the beautiful Marilyn.

Zombie in ripped jeans

STEP 01

Let's start with a simple circle as his head.

STEP 02

After that we'll draw a pentagon for his jaw.

STEP 03

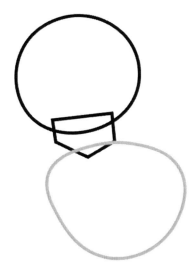

Look at the picture and draw a round shape similar to the one I did. This shape will be the base of his chest.

STEP 04

Draw a curved trapezoid to define his waist.

[98]

STEP 05

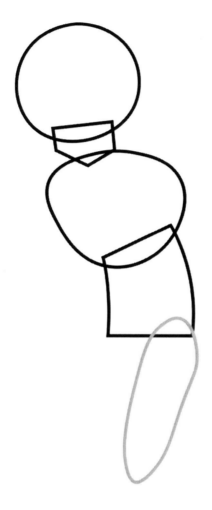

Let's draw his legs. first draw a fat carrot shape as his left thigh;

STEP 06

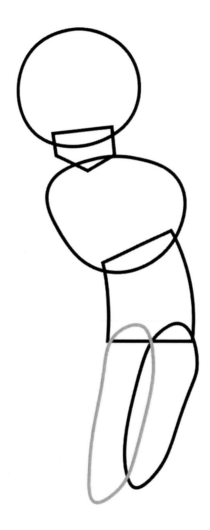

And do the same for the other thigh.

STEP 07

Now add two small circle as his knees.

STEP 08

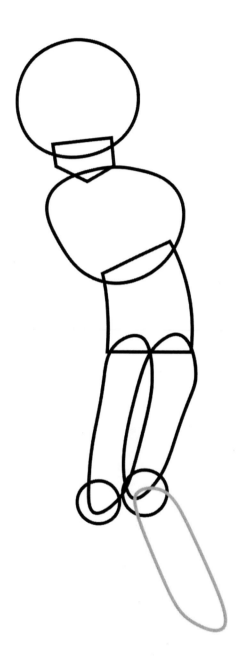

One sausage shape for his left leg;

STEP 09

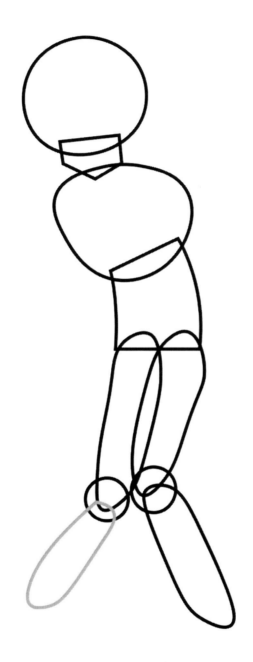

And another one for his right leg.

STEP 10

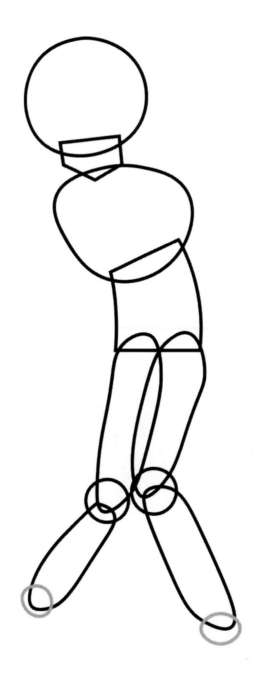

Add two little circles as his ankles.

STEP 11

Draw two potato shapes as the base of his shoes.

STEP 12

It's time to draw his shoulders.

[106]

STEP 13

Draw a carrot shape as his left bicep (his hand is chopped off so you don't have to draw the other parts of his arm).

STEP 14

We will draw his other hand like he's about to catch something.

STEP 15

At this step I have removed some extra lines to show the base shape. You can scape this step if you want to.

STEP 16

We should draw his face at this step.

STEP 17

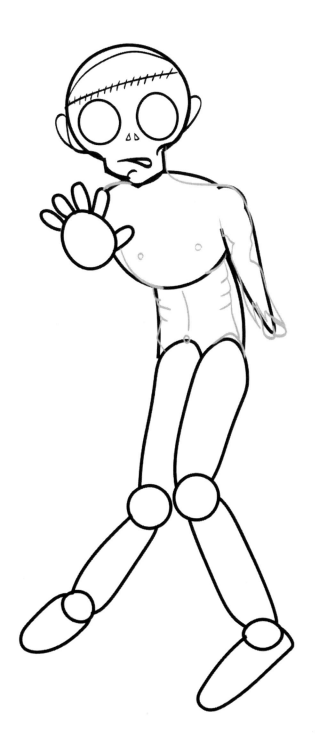

And his upper body as well...

STEP 18

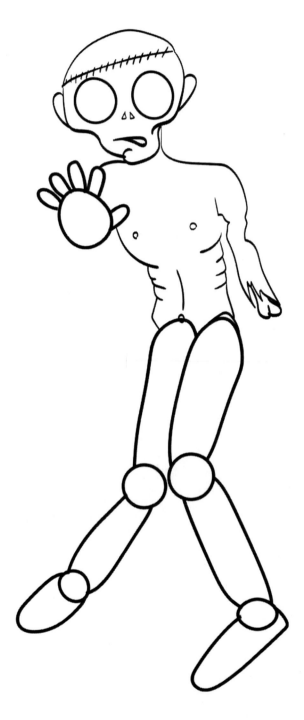

Remove the guide lines of his head and upper body (except his right palm).

STEP 19

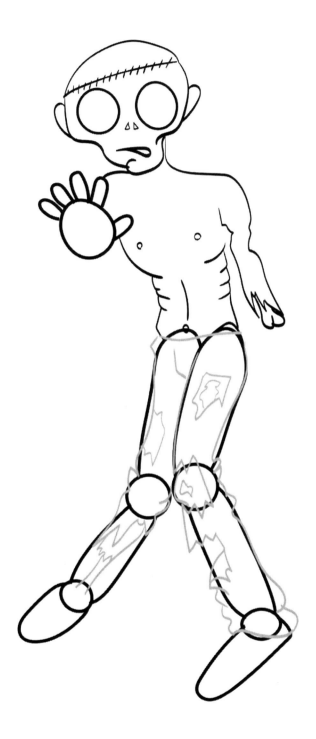

Draw his ripped jeans and legs;

STEP 20

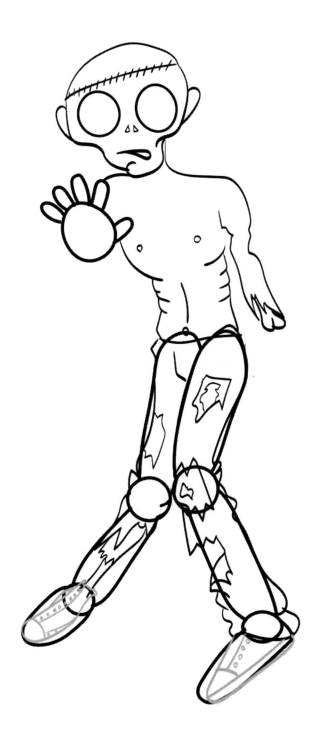

An also his shoes.

STEP 21

Draw his palm and fingers here. Looks like he's chasing some one!

STEP 22

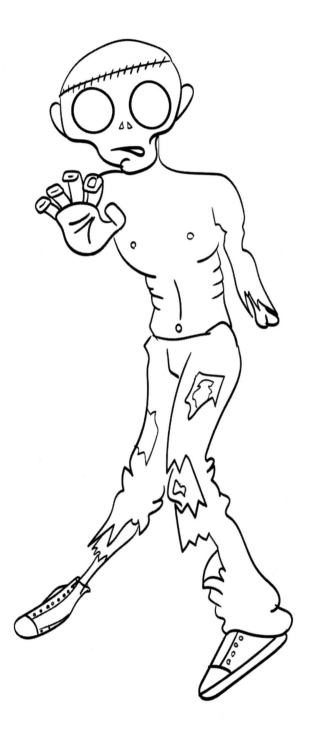

Remove the legs guide lines and we're done.

STEP 23

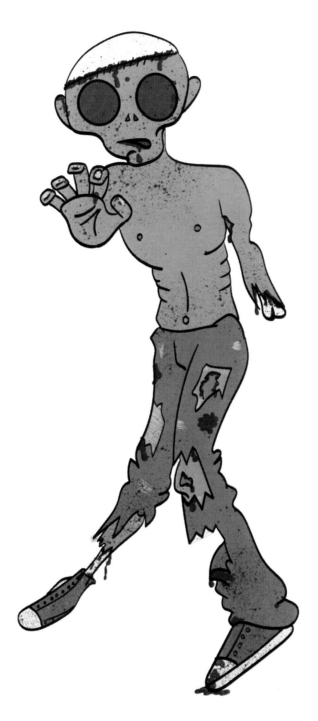

Let's color our drawing. We can draw some blood splashes to make him scarier.

STEP 24

Don't forget the lights and shadows!

STEP 25

As the final step draw a background and your painting is complete!

The Walking dead

STEP 01

As the first step we should draw a circle as his head.

STEP 02

We will draw his jaw and chin right now...

STEP 03

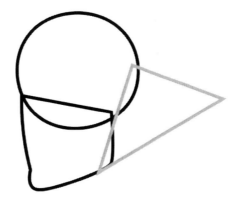

Draw a triangle as you can see as his neck and hump.

STEP 04

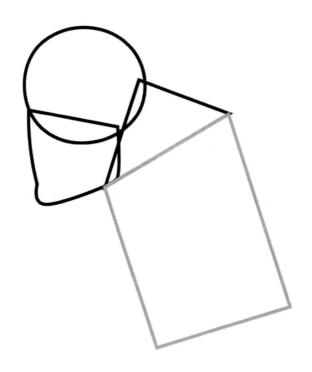

After that add a rectangle as his body;

STEP 05

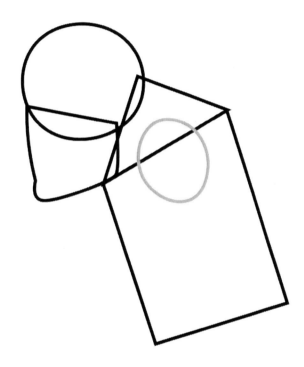

And continue with drawing a circle to define his shoulder.

STEP 06

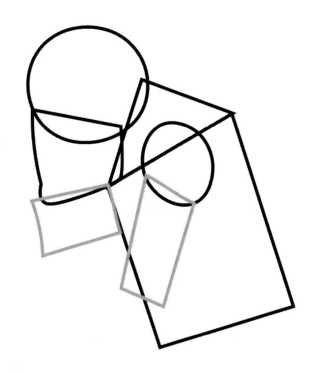

Now we have to draw two rectangles to show his sleeves.

STEP 07

Draw a rectangle as the base shape of his leg;

STEP 08

Do the same for the other leg.

[128]

STEP 09

Two little rectangles as his wrists;

[129]

STEP 10

And another rectangle as his leg.

STEP 11

We should draw his shoe right now.

STEP 12

Draw two rounded shapes as the base shapes of his hands. The base is done as you can see.

STEP 13

We'll draw his face and add some wounds on his head and face.

STEP 14

Erase the extra lines of his head and after that draw his coat.

STEP 15

Let's draw his pants and shoe. I have drawn a bone as his left leg. Don't forget to remove the guide lines of his upper body.

STEP 16

It's time to draw his hand; it looks like he is chasing some one!

STEP 17

Now we'll remove the remaining guide lines and extra lines.

Our art line is ready.

STEP 18

We should color our drawing. I have painted some blood, you can remove that parts if you want to.

STEP 19

Some shadows and highlights go over the suit and body as well.

STEP 20

And finally paint a back ground. You can draw a spooky night with some thunders…

About the Author

Andy Hopper is an American illustrator born in sunny California just a hair's breadth from the beautiful Sierra foothills. After studying Design and Media at UCLA, Andy decided to try his hand at teaching his own unique style of art to novice artists just starting out with their craft.

He has won numerous art awards and has several publications in print and e-book to his credit. His e-books teach the beginner artist how to draw using simple techniques suitable for all ages. While Andy prefers using chalk, pencil and pastels for his own artwork, but has been known to dabble in the world of watercolour from time to time and teach this skill to his students.

Andy Hopper lives just outside of Los Angeles in Santa Monica, California with his wife of 15 years and their three children. His art studio is a welcome respite to the area and he has been known to start impromptu outdoor art sessions with the people in his neighborhood for no charge.

Made in United States
North Haven, CT
26 October 2021